D1295440

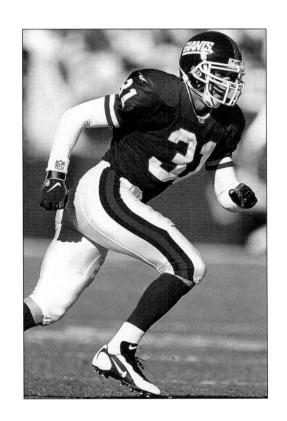

CREATIVE EDUCATION

NEW YORK
GIANTS

JULIE NELSON

Published by Creative Education
123 South Broad Street, Mankato, Minnesota 56001
Creative Education is an imprint of The Creative Company

Designed by Rita Marshall

Photos by: Allsport USA, AP/Wide World Photos, Bettmann/CORBIS,
SportsChrome

Library of Congress Cataloging-in-Publication Data

Nelson, Julie.
New York Giants / by Julie Nelson.
p. cm. — (NFL today)
Summary: Traces the history of the team from its beginnings through 1999.
ISBN 1-58341-052-X

1. New York Giants (Football team)—History—Juvenile literature. [1. New York
Giants (Football team)—History. 2. Football—History.] I. Title. II. Series: NFL
today (Mankato, Minn.)

GV956.N4N45   2000
796.332'64'097471—dc21   99-015752

9 8 7 6 5 4 3 2

The towering figure looking out over New York harbor has a face recognizable around the world. That majestic sight, the Statue of Liberty, has welcomed new arrivals to the United States for more than a century. At the base of the statue is a plaque that bears out the famous invitation to America's newest residents: "Give me your tired, your poor, your huddled masses yearning to be free."

Just across the bay from the statue is Ellis Island, the small speck of land where millions of immigrants first landed. Those immigrants came from nearly every country in the world, and many settled in the first city they came to—New

York. While maintaining their cultural identities, these New York citizens also embraced many American customs, including a love for the game of football.

Since the New York Giants began playing in 1925, fans have had plenty of reasons to love the team. In their first 75 seasons, the Giants have been represented by some of football's greatest stars, including Frank Gifford, Y.A. Tittle, and Lawrence Taylor. They have also brought six world championships home to the city of New York.

1 9 2 5

Businessman Tim Mara bought a pro football franchise for New York.

IN THE BEGINNING

When Tim Mara, the Giants' first owner, bought the team for $500 in 1925, football was mainly a college sport and was played by different rules than it is today. The same players played on both offense and defense, scores were usually low, and running plays made up most of the offensive game. Teams were decked out in high-top shoes, leather helmets, and very little padding. They had tough schedules, sometimes playing up to four games a week. Tickets to a football game cost a dollar apiece—a lot of money in 1925—and players earned about $50 a game.

The rough-and-tumble world of football in the 1920s required football players to be able to live with pain. Red Badgro, an early Giants end, recalled one injury he suffered. "Dr. Joe Alexander was coaching the Giants for Tim Mara when I came to them. I had cut my chin open in practice. I needed 11 stitches to close it up. I just went by his office and he didn't have any of his medical equipment with him, so he got a plain needle and sewing thread out of his drawer and

One of the NFC's top cornerbacks, Jason Sehorn.

Charlie Conerly set new team records with 2,175 passing yards and 22 touchdowns.

sewed up my chin. He liked football more than the practice of medicine, I believe."

Although it had some tough, dedicated players like Badgro, New York had trouble keeping a winning coach. Mara went through three coaches in three years before luring Earl Potteiger to the Giants in 1927. Potteiger racked up an 11–1–1 record in 1927, but he left New York the next year. Mara replaced Potteiger with a former Giants player, Steve Owen. Like many early coaches, Owen both coached and played for the team. Mara gave Owen a long-term contract, and the Giants had their head coach for the next 23 years.

Owen stressed a disciplined defensive game. He was responsible for creating the famed "umbrella" defense: a six-man front, one linebacker, and four defensive backs. As the opposing quarterback dropped back into the pocket, two defensive linemen drove back with him as the defense formed a rough semicircle around him. The modern "4–3" defense used by many teams today grew out of this formation.

After leading his Giants to six division titles and two league championships and running up a 150–100–17 record, Owen gave up his coaching job in 1953. The Hall-of-Famer's 23-year record is still one of the best in pro football history.

THE GIANTS' GLORY YEARS

Jim Lee Howell, who became the New York head coach in 1954, guided the Giants with the help of several outstanding assistant coaches, including Vince Lombardi and Tom Landry. Together with his assistants, Howell turned such potential standouts as Frank Gifford into stars.

Gifford came to the Giants out of the University of Southern California. He was a running back/quarterback with talent, drive, and a never-say-die attitude. "Frank was the body and soul of the team," Howell recalled. "He was the player we went to in the clutch." In 12 seasons with New York, Gifford led the Giants to five division titles. Along the way, he scored 78 touchdowns, including a famous 1956 title game touchdown that gave the Giants the NFL championship over the Chicago Bears.

1 9 5 6

Halfback Frank Gifford gained 1,422 combined yards on runs and pass receptions.

Gifford also played a part in what became known as the Yankee Stadium Classic, a 1958 game that ranks among the NFL's most famous contests. On December 28, 1958, the Giants met the Baltimore Colts in the NFL championship game. The rosters looked like a roll call of football heroes. Fifteen of the players in that game would end up in the Pro Football Hall of Fame. Quarterback Charlie Conerly led the Giants, while the Colts boasted an offense guided by the great Johnny Unitas and featuring receivers Raymond Berry and Lenny Moore.

Although it was a rainy day and the game was not pretty, many football historians still regard the game as one of the greatest in the history of the NFL. Six lost fumbles, a handful of interceptions, and two missed field goals only added to the suspense.

With the Giants leading 17–14 and only three minutes left on the clock, Unitas drove the Colts 73 yards in only three plays. When the Colts' drive stalled, Lou Michels kicked a field goal, sending the game into sudden-death overtime. In the extra quarter, the Colts pushed the ball down the length of the field, then set up their last play to look like a Unitas

David Meggett was a dangerous kick returner.

Powerful defensive end Leonard Marshall.

1 9 6 0

End Kyle Rote led all Giants receivers in catches (42) and yards (750).

pass. As the New York defense fell back, Colts back Alan Ameche plowed through the Giants' line for the winning touchdown. The dejected Giants fell 23–17.

Giants owner Tim Mara, who helped create modern pro football, died only a few weeks later. Mara leadership continued, though, when his sons took over the Giants franchise.

Jim Lee Howell's stint at New York ended in 1960. When Vince Lombardi declined to leave his job as the Green Bay Packers' coach to lead the Giants, New York assistant coach Allie Sherman was promoted instead. Sherman, a brilliant student of the game, saw Charlie Conerly's quarterback skills waning. The coach then traded with San Francisco for quarterback Y.A. (Yelberton Abraham) Tittle, a player the 49ers felt was well past his prime. In 1961, the "old" Tittle led the Giants to a 10–3–1 record and was named the league's Most Valuable Player. Tittle led his team to three straight conference titles, yet the NFL championship eluded the powerful Giants.

While Tittle guarded New York's offense in the early 1960s, linebacker Sam Huff anchored the Giants' defense with his bone-crunching style of play. Huff also had an inventive way with words that made him a hit with fans and sportswriters. Some of his favorite expressions, words such as "blitz," "red dog," and "sack," became a permanent part of pro football's vocabulary.

Despite being a hometown favorite, Huff was traded to the Washington Redskins in 1964. Tittle, his skills finally fading, retired the following year. The double loss hit the Giants hard, and they fell from the top of the NFL to the bottom, finishing the 1964 season at 2–12.

O ver the next 15 years, no team had as many good quarterbacks as did the Giants. Five different head coaches
directed such standouts as Earl Morrall, Norm Snead, Fran
Tarkenton, and Craig Morton. But even the best quarterback
can't create a winning team without a strong defense, something New York desperately needed.

Desperation led the Giants to try anything that might
change their luck, and they moved their home field from the
Polo Grounds to Yankee Stadium to even Yale University.
Nothing seemed to do the trick. In 15 seasons, New York
finished above .500 only twice. Fans began to wonder if the
Giants would ever escape the NFC East cellar.

Quarterback Y.A.
Tittle astounded
fans by passing for
36 touchdowns.

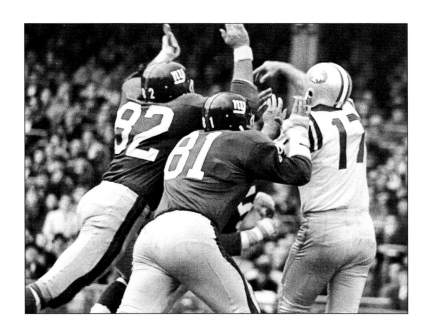

Hall of Fame defensive end Andy Robustelli (#81).

13

The Giants' prospects finally began looking up when George Young came on board in 1979 as general manager. His first job was to hire a head coach. Young looked westward and lured San Diego Chargers assistant coach Ray Perkins to New York.

Young's next acquisition wasn't popular at first with New York fans. Instead of looking to a college football powerhouse for the team's next quarterback, Young and Perkins made unheard-of Morehead State College quarterback Phil Simms their top pick in the 1981 NFL draft.

Simms, an unknown at the time of the draft, would eventually become a key ingredient in the Giants' return to success. But before that could happen, New York needed to do something about its lackluster defense. As it turned out, one of their next draft picks would become one of the most feared and legendary defenders in NFL history. His name was Lawrence Taylor.

1 9 7 9

Ray Perkins took over as the Giants' new head coach, leading them to another 6–10 record.

THE TERROR NAMED TAYLOR

As a child in Williamsburg, Virginia, Lawrence Taylor signed up for a local Jaycees football team. His Jaycees coach, Pete Babcock, said, "Kid, you're going to be a linebacker." That was fine with Taylor, who began studying his new position. "I got books out of the school library on linebackers," Taylor remembered. "I read a lot of stuff about [linebacker greats] Ray Nitschke and Jack Ham and Sam Huff. I read how they saw the game, what their feeling was, what their tempo was. I got this concept right then that, aside from being smart, a good linebacker was also mean."

Halfback Joe Morris starred alongside Phil Simms.

Phil Simms guided New York to victory in Super Bowl XXI.

Years later, Taylor put this education to use as a linebacker for the North Carolina Tar Heels, where his incredible speed and strength made him a dominating force. In game after game, his hustling determination produced big plays for North Carolina. Pro scouts flocked to watch the young star, whose intense style of play would make him a natural fit in the rough-and-tumble world of the NFL.

While Taylor finished college and prepared for the pro ranks, Giants coach Ray Perkins left the pros to coach at the college level in Alabama. Giants management picked Perkins's assistant, Bill Parcells, as head coach. Shortly thereafter, Parcells and the Giants drafted Taylor. New York fans would not be disappointed. During the first week of training camp, Parcells turned to one of his assistants and said, "I gotta get this kid into the game."

Drafting "L.T.," as Taylor was called, turned out to be one of New York's wisest decisions. By the end of his rookie year, Taylor had 9.5 sacks, 94 solo tackles, and 39 assisted stops. Parcells found that Taylor had another talent, too. "What he really did was change the way the other teams looked at our defense," Parcells recalled. "He scared them, is what he did."

Parcells was in an enviable position. He had a superb offensive leader in Phil Simms and a standout defensive presence in Taylor. In 1984, Taylor and Simms maneuvered the Giants into contention for the NFC championship. New York won the Wild Card playoff spot and eked out a 16–13 victory over the Los Angeles Rams in the first round of the postseason. In the NFC title game, however, 49ers quarterback Joe Montana escaped Taylor's clutches enough times to lead San Francisco to the title.

1 9 8 2

Linebacker Harry Carson made three quarterback sacks and solidified New York's run defense.

Lawrence Taylor's speed as a pass rusher was legendary (pages 18-19).

Joe Morris exploded for a franchise-record 21 rushing touchdowns.

The Giants knew that it would take nothing less than their best effort to reach the Super Bowl. In 1985, though, the Giants weren't at their best. Although they didn't reach the Super Bowl, they did make it to the playoffs. That was the good news. The bad news was that L.T. was having problems with substance abuse.

Alcohol and drug abuse brings careers to an end for many athletes, but L.T. was determined to beat his problem. With faith in his own strength, Taylor began receiving treatment. When L.T. returned to the Giants, he was determined to resume his dominant ways, vowing to make 1986 his best year yet. He didn't let his team down.

The Giants seemed unbeatable that season. Phil Simms was passing to perfection, and Phil McConkey proved to be one of the league's most dangerous receivers. On defense, Taylor again made his presence felt as he terrorized opposing quarterbacks. He collected 20.5 sacks, close to a new league record, and was named the NFL's Most Valuable Player. He joined only one other defensive player, the great Alan Page, in winning this high honor.

Taylor's teammates were also making and breaking records. Running back Joe Morris broke his own Giants single-season record, rushing for 1,516 yards. Tight end Mark Bavaro caught 66 passes for 1,001 yards, setting another franchise record. As a team, the Giants tied the Chicago Bears with a 14–2 mark for the best record in the league.

In the playoffs, the Giants continued their remarkable winning streak. They rolled over San Francisco 49–3 and Washington 17–0, earning the right to meet the Denver Broncos in the Super Bowl.

That Super Bowl would became a personal showcase for Simms and McConkey. "Conk," as McConkey's teammates affectionately nicknamed him, had begun standing on the sideline bench during the regular season and waving a towel to encourage New York fans to get up out of their seats to cheer on the Giants.

McConkey continued his towel-waving antics in the Super Bowl, and both teammates and fans continued to respond. Simms completed a remarkable 22 of 25 passes, breaking the Super Bowl record with an 88 percent pass completion mark. His second-half completion of 10 straight passes set another record. Behind Simms's near-perfect performance, the Giants beat the Broncos 39–20. Simms was named the Super Bowl MVP, and New York was at last on top of the NFL.

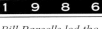

Bill Parcells led the Giants to a 14–2 record and was named NFL Coach of the Year.

Sure-handed tight end Mark Bavaro.

However, the Giants found that success came and went quickly. Football commissioner Pete Rozelle announced that the league would use new methods to bring "parity" to the NFL. He and team owners put together tougher schedules for the top teams, making competition stiffer for the winners and easier for the weaker teams. After 1986, it became much more difficult for teams to repeat as Super Bowl champs.

Besides the parity rule, the Giants were also plagued with player problems in 1987 and '88. Lawrence Taylor had recurring personal problems, Mark Bavaro was involved in a bitter contract dispute, nine-time Pro-Bowl linebacker Harry Carson retired, and injuries hit the Giants hard.

1 9 8 7

Phil McConkey set a team record with nine punt returns in a single game.

INTO THE 1990S

In 1989, the Giants returned to the playoffs mainly through hard work. "We don't have the stars we had on the Super Bowl team," Lawrence Taylor said. "We have a bunch of guys who are just hard workers, guys who want it." Taylor was talking about the young players who were bringing a new generation of leadership to the Giants.

Coach Parcells began shifting the Giants' philosophy toward ball control. "I knew the game was changing," he said. "There are too many multiple defenses nowadays—too many different fronts. You can't run eight different schemes against eight different fronts. You're better off just lining up with your big guys and pounding away."

With this plan in mind, Parcells began stocking up on powerful offensive linemen, drafting Eric Moore, Jumbo Elliot, Brian Williams, and Bob Kratch. Parcells hoped that his

Rodney Hampton produced much of the Giants' offense, gaining 1,059 rushing yards.

big front line would give Simms more time to calculate his passing and would open up holes for Giants runners.

Parcells's strategy worked as the Giants finished with a 12–4 record and their second NFC Eastern Division championship in four years. Veteran running back Ottis Anderson, filling in for an injured Joe Morris, rushed for 1,023 yards. Rookie runner David Meggett also set a Giants record with 582 yards in punt returns. The Giants continued their victorious ways in 1990, starting the season with a 10-game winning streak and finishing with a 13–3 record and another NFC East championship.

In the playoffs, New York demolished Chicago 31–3, squeaked by San Francisco 15–13, and went on to meet Buffalo in Super Bowl XXV. Jeff Hostetler, filling in at quarterback for an injured Phil Simms, tossed a 14-yard touchdown pass to Stephen Baker in the second quarter, but Buffalo held a 12–10 lead at halftime. In the third quarter, the Giants put together a 14-play drive that culminated in a one-yard touchdown run by Ottis Anderson. Kicker Matt Bahr added a second field goal, and the Giants eked out a 20–19 victory to give them their second Super Bowl triumph in five years.

In the aftermath of the Super Bowl victory came some major changes in the team's management. After 65 years of ownership, the Mara family sold its share of the team. The Giants also lost their coach when Bill Parcells resigned.

For the next two years, injuries plagued the unlucky Giants, knocking them from their championship level. Quarterbacks Jeff Hostetler and Phil Simms were often sidelined with various ailments, and Lawrence Taylor injured his Achilles tendon in a 1992 game against Green Bay. Although he returned to play for one more season, Taylor would never regain the dominant form that made him the NFL's most feared man.

The Giants' poor records in 1991 and 1992 led management to bring in former Denver Broncos coach Dan Reeves. Coach Reeves, who had led the Broncos to three Super Bowl appearances, eagerly accepted the challenge of making the Giants contenders again. In his first year, Reeves guided the Giants to an 11–5 regular-season record and a 17–10 Wild Card game victory over Minnesota. Unfortunately, New York next faced the powerful San Francisco 49ers and were crushed 44–3.

1 9 9 3

Offensive tackle John (Jumbo) Elliott was named to the Pro Bowl for the first time.

Reeves took the team through a roller-coaster 1994 schedule that began with three straight wins, ended with six straight wins, but added up to a regular-season record of only 9–7. By the end of 1994, both Lawrence Taylor and Phil Simms were no longer in Giants jerseys. An era had ended.

STANDING TALL

Although New York fans had good reason to expect brighter years in the late 1990s with powerful rusher Rodney Hampton and deep-threat receiver Chris Calloway leading the way, the Giants struggled the next two seasons, finishing 5–11 in 1995 and 6–10 in 1996. New York had a solid defensive lineup, but its offense sputtered, finishing last in the NFL in 1996.

Giants management elected to make a change at the top in 1997 and brought in Jim Fassel as the team's new head coach. Fassel, a former Giants assistant, embraced the chal-

Powerful rusher Rodney Hampton (pages 26-27).

lenge of leading the historic franchise out of the NFC Eastern Division basement.

Although 1997 started badly for the Giants—with a 1–3 record and a season-ending eye injury to standout center Brian Williams—Fassel refused to make drastic changes. "That little red panic button is always there if you want to reach up and push it," he said. "But I would have lost them right then if I started making wholesale changes. . . . Everything I'd have told them about being consistent and staying the course would have gone out the window."

Fassel's courage paid off, and the Giants turned things around, finishing the season 10–5–1 and capturing the NFC East title. The new coach had done the unthinkable—leading the Giants from last place in the division to first in only

1 9 9 5

Dave Brown had his best season as the Giants' quarterback, passing for 2,814 yards.

Deep-threat receiver Chris Calloway.

one season. "The biggest thing we've done was getting these guys to have a mental toughness," Fassel explained. "We changed our attitude into more of a 'can-do' mode."

Once again, the Giants' defense was one of the strongest in the league. Linebacker Jessie Armstead set a franchise record with 134 total tackles, and powerful defensive end Michael Strahan finished third in the NFL with 14 sacks.

Unfortunately, the celebration would end in heartbreaking fashion. In the first round of the playoffs, the Giants hosted the Wild Card Minnesota Vikings. New York led 19–3 at halftime. As the game wound down, New York's tough defense continued to hold down the Vikings, and with only two minutes remaining, the Giants held what looked like a comfortable 22–13 lead.

However, Vikings quarterback Randall Cunningham drove the Minnesota offense the length of the field for a touchdown, cutting the lead to 22–20 with a minute left. The Vikings then recovered an onside kick. Several passes and an interference call later, Minnesota kicker Eddie Murray drilled a game-winning field goal to end both the game and the Giants' comeback season.

In 1998, the Giants slipped back to a disappointing 8–8 record. Newly acquired running back Gary Brown took over for the departed Rodney Hampton by rushing for 1,063 yards. But the absence of key players—Williams out with an eye injury and top cornerback Jason Sehorn out with a knee injury—again deflated the team's chances.

Despite losing defensive end Chad Bratzke and receiver Chris Calloway in the off-season, the Giants were confident they could return to their playoff ways in 1999. In an effort

1 9 9 9

Receiver Ike Hilliard used his great quickness to rack up a career-high 996 yards.

Linebacker Jessie Armstead hit with crushing force.

All-Pro defensive end Michael Strahan.

Micheal Barrow was expected to strengthen a solid linebacker corps.

to stabilize their offense, the Giants acquired Kerry Collins, a young quarterback with proven numbers and a troubled past. Collins had proven himself with two solid seasons in Carolina before a rocky 1997 led to his release.

Collins proved to be an excellent gamble for the Giants, as he teamed with receivers Amani Toomer and Ike Hilliard to lead New York's offense. Collins threw for nearly 300 yards in three of his last five starts, but his efforts were not enough. After a 5–3 start, the Giants struggled down the stretch and missed the playoffs for a second straight year.

After the season, the Giants added considerable firepower to their lineup by drafting huge running back Ron Dayne out of the University of Wisconsin. New York fans hoped that the 255-pound Dayne—who won the Heisman Trophy after becoming the NCAA's all-time leading rusher—would finally give the Giants a consistent running attack. "One of the things we really liked is the way he takes over in the fourth quarter," said personnel director Marv Sunderland. "He keeps coming at you and coming at you, and pretty soon he wears you out."

Since 1925, the Giants have truly been a towering force in the NFL. The team has won world championships in five different decades and plans to continue that dominance in the 21st century. To Giants fans, there is no more fitting place for football's biggest trophy than the "Big Apple."